THE HAPPY BIRT

Can you remember
grandma's parrot's
date man first landed on the moon? Do
you know what happened on Gyles
Brandreth's worst birthday? Or Gary
Wilmot's best birthday ever?

With this ultimate write-in birthday
book you'll soon know everything you
need to about birthdays. Happy
Birthday reading!

ALISON GRAHAM has celebrated her birthday for as long as she can remember. It is always on the same day each year when she hosts a party for all her friends. If this book was given to you on *your* birthday, Alison would like to take this opportunity to wish you Many Happy Returns of the Day!

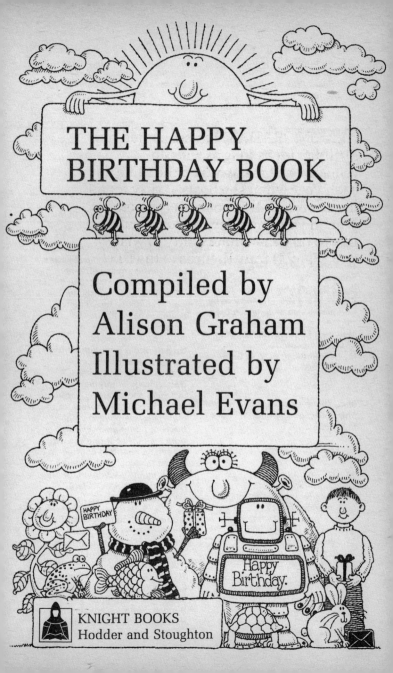

THE HAPPY BIRTHDAY BOOK

Compiled by
Alison Graham
Illustrated by
Michael Evans

KNIGHT BOOKS
Hodder and Stoughton

My Best – and Worst – Birthday, © Gyles Brandreth, 1989
My Worst Birthday and An Emergency Present, © Mary Danby, 1989
My Worst Birthday, © Terrance Dicks, 1989
Patty and Mildred Hill, reproduced by permission of Keith Prowse Music Pub Co Ltd., London WC2H 0EA
The Birthday Present, © Margaret Mahy, 1977, from *Nonstop Nonsense*, reproduced by kind permission of J. M. Dent
Between Birthdays, © Ogden Nash, from *The New Nutcracker Suite*, reproduced by kind permission of Curtis Brown, London
The Perfect Host, © Tony Robinson, 1989
Dog's Day, © Shel Silverstein, from *A Light in the Attic*, reproduced by kind permission of Jonathan Cape, 1982
Monday's Child (revised version), © Joan Stimson, 1989
My Best Birthday Ever, © Gary Wilmot, 1989

Illustrations © Michael Evans, 1989
This collection © Signpost Books Ltd., 1989

First published in Great Britain in 1989 by Knight Books

British Library C.I.P.

Graham, Alison
 The happy birthday book.
 1. Celebrities. Birthdays
 I. Graham, Alison
 920.'02

 ISBN 0-340-50184-7

The characters and situations in this book are entirely imaginary and bear no relation to any real person or actual happening.

Printed and bound in Great Britain for Hodder and Stoughton Paperbacks, a division of Hodder and Stoughton Limited, Mill Road, Dunton Green, Sevenoaks, Kent TN13 2YA (Editorial Office: 47 Bedford Square, London WC1B 3DP) by Richard Clay Limited, Bungay, Suffolk. Photoset by Rowland Phototypesetting Limited, Bury St Edmunds, Suffolk.

CONTENTS

My birthday

MY BIRTHDAY IS ON ....

I shall be ...... years old

My full name is ....

My address is ....

....

My school is ....

My sign of the Zodiac is ....

Me when I was a baby   Me now

I was born at (address) ....

and the time was ....

The most special thing about my birthday is ....

....

MY WORST BIRTHDAY
by Terrance Dicks

I can't honestly say I remember the day I'm going to tell you about but I know all about it just the same.

It happened when I was very young and it became a sort of family legend. One of those embarrassing stories dragged out year after year, as shaming as your baby picture nude on a bearskin rug.

You might not think it to look at me now – in fact, to be perfectly honest, you definitely *wouldn't* think it to look at me now – but I was an exceptionally beautiful baby.

I even won second prize in a Beautiful Baby Contest on Canvey Island.

I grew up into an equally beautiful toddler, with big brown eyes and lots of curly brown hair.

Mum was potty about me, the way new mums are. I had the biggest and shiniest pram in the street and a collection of fancy baby clothes that you wouldn't believe.

On my second birthday Mum decided to have a big party to show me off.

She dressed me up in a white silk suit that would have made Little Lord Fauntleroy feel sick.

(There was a faded family photograph of me in this revolting outfit around for years. It's lost now, thank goodness. Heaven help me if my kids ever find it again.)

Anyway, there I was on the big day, sitting in the seldom-used Best Front Room surrounded by an assortment of local toddlers, all scrubbed and grizzling and waiting to get their hands on the cake and jelly.

Mum had invited some rather snooty lady from the posh end of the street, some sort of local Lady Bountiful. Whoever she was, she didn't really know our family very well.

Otherwise she'd never have made the Fatal Mistake.

She swept in rather late, and saw me enthroned in my high chair, a vision in white silk suit and curly brown ringlets.

Leaning over me, she ruffled my curls and gushed, 'What a *sweet* little girl!'

So I spat in her eye.

Well, you would, wouldn't you?

Uproar! Shame and disgrace! I got slapped, I roared, all the other kids roared in sympathy.

Not long after that Mum got me a haircut and some decent, ordinary clothes.

Sometimes I think of it as my finest hour . . .

In fact, I think it inspired my Ghastly Party Tip:

Hope for the best, prepare for the worst and don't stand any nonsense from people who think they're your betters.

Works quite well for life as a whole really . . .

MY BEST PRESENTS

The present I would like most this year is ....
....

The best present I have ever had was ....
....

The best present I could ever have would be ....
....

The best present I got this year was ....
....

given to me by ....

The biggest present I had was ....
....

from ....

The tiniest present I had was ....
....

from ....

The prettiest present I had was ....
....

from ....

I had .... presents this year

Other best present facts ....
....

My birthday diary last year.

LAST YEAR I WAS .... YEARS OLD

My birthday was on a .... (day of the week)

The weather was ....

I had .... presents

I had .... cards

What I did that day was ....

What I remember best was ....

During last year the best thing that happened to me
was ....

The worst thing that happened last year was ....

....

MY BIRTHDAY IS ON .... (day)

The weather ....

Today I ....

....

....

....

The best thing that happened was ....

....

People who came to my party ....

....

People who sent me cards ....

....

People who gave me presents ....

....

I felt .... today

The things I want to remember about today are ....

....

I got up at .... and went to bed at ....

12

MY BIRTHDAY DIARY – NEXT YEAR

Next year I will be .... years old

My birthday will be on a .... (day)

The things I would like to do most on my birthday are ....

....

The people I would most like to invite to my party are ....

....

The presents I would like to get most are ....

....

The thing I'd most like to change by next year is ....

....

The things I hope to achieve during the year are ......

....

When I am ...., I shall be old enough to ....

....

If I could make one wish on my birthday next year it would be ....

....

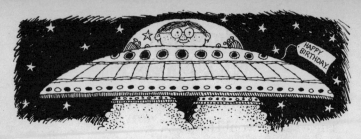

MY BIRTHDAY DIARY – SOMETIME

The age I most look forward to being is ....

I shall be able to do ....

I hope I will have achieved ....

For this birthday, I will celebrate by ....

What I would like to happen is ....

People I would like to invite to my party are ....

....

The presents I would like to have sometime are ....

....

The birthday treat I would like to have sometime
is ....

....

If I were king or queen for that day I would rule
that ....

....

The rule I would most like to abolish sometime is ..

....

If I could have one talent just for one birthday, I'd
choose ....

MY BIRTHDAY DIARY – NEVER

The birthday I don't want to have is ....

The weather would be ....

I never want to be given presents like ....

....

The sort of food I never want to have at a party is ......

....

I would never wear clothes like ....

I may never be able to ....,
but I'd love to try!

THINGS I'D LIKE TO GET

The presents I'd most like to have are ....

The animal I'd most like to have as a pet is ....

....

The food I'd most like to eat is ....

If I had three wishes, they would be for ....

....

If I had one magical present, it would be ....

....

If I could celebrate my birthday any way I wanted,
I'd ....

....

If I could have any character from a book at my
party, I'd invite ....

If I could invite one famous person to my party, I'd
choose ....

HAPPY BIRTHDAY.

THINGS I'D HATE TO GET

These are presents I definitely don't want this year .

....

The worst present I ever had was ....

................, because ....

The most boring present I ever had was ....

................, because ....

Things I never want to be given are ....

....

The worst present any of my friends has been given
was ....

....

given to ....

The worst present I ever gave anybody was ....

The hardest thank-you letter I ever had to write was
for ....

MONDAY'S CHILD
(revised version)

Monday's child is late for school,
Tuesday's child just plays the fool.
Wednesday's child is on a diet,
Thursday's child has caused a riot.
Friday's child eats fish with jelly,
Saturday's child's in love with telly.
But the child who is born on the Sabbath
day
Is laid back, cool and rules . . . okay?

Joan Stimson

WHAT I'D LIKE TO FIND INSIDE ON MY BIRTHDAY

Draw what you'd like.

My family's birthday.

MY MOTHER ....

MY FATHER ....

MY BROTHERS ....

....

MY SISTERS ....

....

MY AUNTS ....

....

MY UNCLES ....

....

MY COUSINS ....

....

MY GRANDMOTHERS ....

....

MY GRANDFATHERS ....

....

20

OTHER FAMILY BIRTHDAYS

NAME	BIRTHDAY

MY FRIENDS' BIRTHDAYS!

THE FRIEND I HAVE KNOWN LONGEST IS ....

....

BIRTHDAY ....

MY FRIENDS IN SCHOOL ARE

(name) .... (birthday) ....

(name) .... (birthday) ....

(name) .... (birthday) ....

(name) .... (birthday) ....

(name) .... (birthday) ....

MY FRIENDS OUT OF SCHOOL ARE

(name) .... (birthday) ....

(name) .... (birthday) ....

(name) .... (birthday) ....

(name) .... (birthday) ....

(name) .... (birthday) ....

Presents I have given my friends this year ....

....

....

The person I'd most like to make friends with is ......

.... (birthday) ....

The character in a book I'd most like to make friends
with is ....

(birthday) .... (guess if you don't know)

Presents I'd like to give my friends ....

....

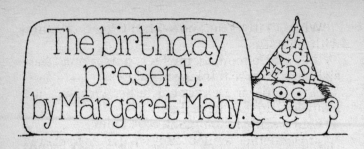

The birthday present. by Margaret Mahy.

One morning a word wizard was walking home from a successful all-night wizards' party given to open the Monster Sale at the Wizards' Bargain Stores. He heard voices coming through an open window. Mr and Mrs Delmonico were having breakfast and discussing important business. The word wizard, who liked to know about other people's business, stopped and listened carefully.

'Our dear twins are growing up,' sighed Mrs Delmonico. 'Sarah is so dashing with her beautiful black curls and shining eyes, and Francis is every bit her equal. He says he wants to be an astronomer and study comets. Do you think that is a good career for a boy?'

'I would rather he went into an estate agency,' Mr Delmonico replied. 'There is a lot of money in land.'

'And what shall we give the twins for their birthday?' Mrs Delmonico went on. 'What about a pet of some kind? Children love a pet.'

Mr Delmonico did not want his twins, Sarah and Francis to have pets, but he did not like to argue with his wife. He decided to get his own way by cunning.

'What a good idea!' he exclaimed. 'I wish I could have ideas like yours, my dear. What sort of pet do you have in mind?'

'A pony, perhaps,' Mrs Delmonico said doubtfully, but her husband said:

'What a pity! You know I can't stand creatures with eight legs.'

'But, Mr Delmonico, my love, horses don't have eight legs. You're thinking of spiders.'

'Oh!' said Mr Delmonico rather crossly, 'how many legs do they have then?'

'Four each,' Mrs Delmonico told him.

Mr Delmonico smiled. 'But we'd have to get two ponies – one for Sarah and one for Francis. Two horses with four legs each. That makes eight, I'm sure you'll agree, my dear.'

'Oh, goodness me, yes, so it does,' sighed Mrs Delmonico.

('This man is a very tricky customer!' thought the word wizard, listening carefully.)

'Well then, what about a dog?' asked Mrs Delmonico.

'A dog!' muttered Mr Delmonico pretending to consider. 'The trouble with dogs is their barking.'

'Oh Mr Delmonico, a dog's bark is harmless.'

'No,' Mr Delmonico replied quickly, 'I understand a dog's bark can be worse than his bite, and not only that – dogs are well known for barking up the wrong tree. I don't think a dog would suit this family. We've got so many trees in the garden the poor dog would wear himself out trying to find the right tree to bark up. No. I don't think a dog would do.'

'Well, what about a kitten?' asked Mrs Delmonico, crunching toast daintily. 'Kittens are pretty and, besides, they're a good investment. Cats have nine lives, you know.'

'True! True!' answered Mr Delmonico, sipping his hot coffee. 'But they have their disadvantages. You know how any music on the violin brings on my hay fever.'

'But dear, what does a violin have to do with a

kitten for the twins?'

'Don't you remember, "Hey diddle diddle, the cat and the fiddle"?' Mr Delmonico cried.

'But, dear Mr Delmonico, that was only one cat,' his wife protested.

'If one can play the fiddle they all can,' Mr Delmonico declared. 'I don't fancy taking the risk. Besides they're so everyday and all over the place, cats. How about something more unusual?'

'What do you say to a lion, then?' Mrs Delmonico asked. 'Lions are very beautiful and very brave. There is a well-known saying, "As bold as a lion".'

'Oh my dear,' Mr Delmonico exclaimed laughing, 'the real saying is, "Bald as a lion". Lions are only beautiful to begin with. On their second birthdays they suddenly go instantaneously bald, and the chairs and the carpets are covered in lion hair.'

Mrs Delmonico supped a cup of tea in a disappointed fashion. 'I should hate that,' she said. 'Perhaps we'd better get the twins a pet next year.'

'Goodness me, what a woman you are for good ideas,' cried Mr Delmonico. 'You are very wise, my dear. Leave the twins' birthday presents to me.'

('Well,' thought the wizard, 'here's a man who uses words for the purposes of confustication. Here's a man who chops words and changes meanings. A word wizard can't stand for that. I'll teach him a lesson. Let me see now – what can I contrive?')

The wizard tossed an idea into the air. It buzzed off like a mosquito, over the lawn straight to Mr Delmonico and stung him on the end of his nose.

Mr Delmonico brought his twins, Sarah and Francis, presents beginning with 'C', like cameras and crayons, clarinets and comics, and a great big fire-engine-red Christmas cracker. It had a black label on it, saying:

'Beware. Monster Cracker.'

'I bought it at the Wizards' Bargain Store Monster Sale,' Mr Delmonico said. 'I can't wait to see what's inside it.'

Francis took one end and Sarah took the other. They pulled and they pulled and they pulled and they pulled, and then, suddenly, the cracker burst with a snap and a roar like a cannon let off in a cave full of echoes. The room filled with smoke and the smell of gunpowder.

But when the smoke cleared away, there, sitting in the middle of the floor, was a monster.

It had eight legs and carried a violin tucked under its chin. It wore a collar and tie and had a hundred teeth all sharp. It had horns and hairy ears, but the top of its head was quite bald. It smiled at Sarah and Francis and barked.

'A monster! A monster!' cried the twins. 'At last we've got a pet. Thank you, thank you, darling father.'

Mr Delmonico had to let them keep it, of course, but he couldn't help feeling that someone had got the better of him after all.

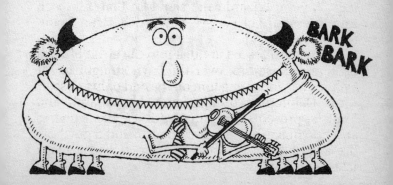

AN EMERGENCY PRESENT
a useful tip from Mary Danby

It's Sunday . . . You've been invited to a birthday party
. . . You've forgotten to buy a present . . . And the shops
are shut.

Don't panic.

Find a small box or jar. Cover it with pretty paper. Tie a
label round it: 'Lucky Dip'.

Now go round the house and see what you can find to
put in it.

Suggestions: A wrapped sweet or two, a paperclip, an
unused eraser, a wrapped chocolate biscuit, a sticker, a
small bar of soap (or any small toiletries), a few small toys
(in good condition), dice, a marble, a hair clip etc. etc.

It may not be the smartest present, but it'll probably be
the most unusual.

JUMBLED WORDS

Can you unjumble these words? *Clue*: they are all to do with birthdays!

NSEEPTSR

NCOEILTEABR

RNDFSIE

SSSAAUGE

PPGNARSWI

HDSBYITAR

EAKC

FGSTI

RAEISTP

EEGGSITRN SDCRA

LRPSEAC

VOLEPEEN

ALOHETOCC

YRRAASVEINN

TTTEEENNNIARM

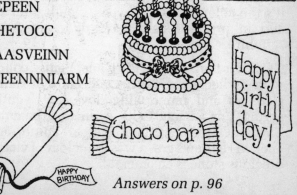

Answers on p. 96

LUCKY COLOURS

Did you know that colours all have special meanings? Throughout history, and all over the world, different colours have represented special qualities, or have special associations.

BLACK is associated with the planet Saturn, which astrologers connect with the Zodiac signs Aquarius and Capricorn. It can mean prudence, wisdom, and constancy: time and the number 8. American Indians think of it as the colour of Night, and the Chinese regard it as having to do with winter, water, and the tortoise. Ancient Egyptians thought black was the colour of rebirth and resurrection. In precious stones it's represented by the diamond.

BLUE stands for hope, sincerity, truth, faithfulness and peace. In the Zodiac it's related to the planet Jupiter, allied to Pisces and Sagittarius. Buddhists see blue as representing the coolness of the heavens above and the waters below, while for ancient Celts it was the colour of bards and poets. For the Chinese it's the colour of the heavens, clouds, and spring, and in precious stones it's represented by the sapphire.

GREEN is the colour of the planet Venus, connected with Zodiac signs Taurus and Libra. It stands for gladness and immortality, love, joy, youth and spring. For ancient Celts green was the colour of Tir-na-nOg, the Land of Eternal Youth, and for ancient Hebrews green was the colour of victory. Its precious stone is an emerald.

PURPLE is the royal colour, and shows pomp, justice, and temperance. It's the colour of the planet Mercury (Virgo and Gemini). The Aztecs and the Incas in America saw it as the colour of majesty and sovereignty, and for Christians it's not only the royal colour but also stands for truth, humility and penitence.
The precious stone is amethyst.

RED is often thought to be a masculine colour, having to do with war and warlike things. It is connected with energy, fire, health, strength, festivity, magnanimity and fortitude. American Indians thought of the red of day, and for the Chinese it's the colour of the sun, fire, summer, and the south – the luckiest of all colours. For the ancient Celts, however, it meant death and disaster, and Hebrews saw it as the colour of severity. In classical Rome, the faces of gods were often painted red, to show divinity. The red planet is Mars, which controls Scorpio and Aries, and the special precious stone is ruby.

Black

WHITE is for purity, innocence, hope, and birth into new life. Many religions have regarded white as the colour of holiness, and it's worn at both weddings and funerals. It can also mean friendship and goodwill. In Chinese lore, it's the colour of the White Tiger, of the West, and of autumn, and the ancient Egyptians saw it, together with green, as the colour of joy. For Hindus it means self-illumination and light, and amongst Maoris it's the colour of truce. Christians use it for major festivals, like Christmas and Easter. The white planet is the Moon (or Diana, the Roman name), which rules Cancer. The precious stone is the pearl.

YELLOW is Apollo's colour, the classical god of the Sun, and the Zodiac sign is Leo. It stands for glory, light, intuition, faith and goodness. The saffron-yellow robes of Buddhist monks symbolise renunciation and humility, and the Chinese regard yellow as the colour of the Earth and of the hare in the moon. In Hebrew lore it means beauty, and for Hindus it stands for light, life, truth and immortality. Yellow is represented by the precious stone topaz.

Yellow

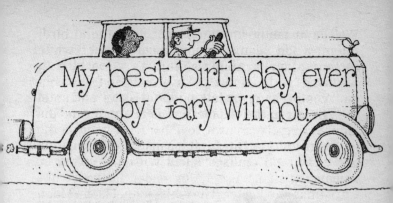

My best birthday ever by Gary Wilmot

On the morning of my last birthday, I awoke to find my wife and daughters standing by my bed with a tray of champagne, orange juice and lots of goodies and singing 'Happy Birthday to You'.

My wife then put the most comfortable pillows behind my back so that I could sit up comfortably and drink my Bucks Fizz and eat the various goodies as well. Following a relaxing breakfast I was despatched to my bathroom where a hot bath had been run for me, my dressing gown and slippers awaiting me.

Having finished this luxurious bath and lazily dressing, I was led to the front gate where my wife was waiting with suitcases and a chauffeur-driven car to take us all to the airport for a flight to Barbados. On arrival in Barbados, the five star hotel we were to stay in had laid on a chauffeur-driven Rolls Royce to take us there. This journey was only hampered by the thousands of people waiting to greet me and to tear at my clothing.

We then spent a luxurious two weeks, during which time the local politicians and celebrities visited and my every wish was seen to instantly.

When the time came to return home, I woke up

on the morning and having got used to the 'treatment' I had been receiving, I called out 'Carol, I presume you have laid everything on,' to which she replied:

'Whatever are you talking about Gary?' and I said:

'The car to the airport, and is my bath run,' and she replied:

'Have you gone stark raving mad?' and then – and only then – I realised I had woken up from my dreams.

DOG'S DAY

They could have sung me just one song
To kind of sort of celebrate.
Or left a present on the lawn –
A juicy bone, a piece of steak –
Instead of just a candle on
This lump of dog food on my plate.
But no one cares when a dog is born,
And this ain't much of a birthday cake.

Shel Silverstein

JANUARY

1st	16th ....
2nd	17th ....
3rd	18th ....
4th	19th ....
5th	20th ....
6th	21st ....
7th	22nd ....
8th	23rd ....
9th	24th ....
10th	25th ....
11th	26th ....
12th	27th ....
13th	28th ....
14th	29th ....
15th	30th ....
31st	

FEBRUARY

1st ....

2nd ....

3rd ....

4th ....

5th ....

6th ....

7th ....

8th ....

9th ....

10th ....

11th ....

12th ....

13th ....

14th ....

15th ....

16th ....

17th ....

18th ....

19th ....

20th ....

21st ....

22nd ....

23rd ....

24th ....

25th ....

26th ....

27th ....

28th ....

29th ....

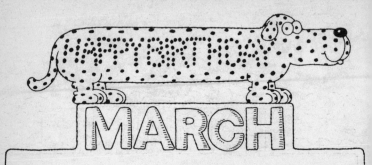

MARCH

1st	16th ....
2nd	17th ....
3rd	18th ....
4th	19th ....
5th	20th ....
6th	21st ....
7th	22nd ....
8th	23rd ....
9th	24th ....
10th	25th ....
11th	26th ....
12th	27th ....
13th	28th ....
14th	29th ....
15th	30th ....
	31st ....

1st	16th ....
2nd	17th ....
3rd	18th ....
4th	19th ....
5th	20th ....
6th	21st ....
7th	22nd ....
8th	23rd ....
9th	24th ....
10th	25th ....
11th	26th ....
12th	27th ....
13th	28th ....
14th	29th ....
15th	30th ....

MAY

1st	16th ....
2nd	17th ....
3rd	18th ....
4th	19th ....
5th	20th ....
6th	21st ....
7th	22nd ....
8th	23rd ....
9th	24th ....
10th	25th ....
11th	26th ....
12th	27th ....
13th	28th ....
14th	29th ....
15th	30th ....

31st ....

Happy birthday

JUNE

1st	16th ....
2nd	17th ....
3rd	18th ....
4th	19th ....
5th	20th ....
6th	21st ....
7th	22nd ....
8th	23rd ....
9th	24th ....
10th	25th ....
11th	26th ....
12th	27th ....
13th	28th ....
14th	29th ....
15th	30th ....

1st ....
2nd ....
3rd ....
4th ....
5th ....
6th ....
7th ....
8th ....
9th ....
10th ....
11th ....
12th ....
13th ....
14th ....
15th ....

16th ....
17th ....
18th ....
19th ....
20th ....
21st ....
22nd ....
23rd ....
24th ....
25th ....
26th ....
27th ....
28th ....
29th ....
30th ....

31st ....

AUGUST

1st	16th ....
2nd	17th ....
3rd	18th ....
4th	19th ....
5th	20th ....
6th	21st ....
7th	22nd ....
8th	23rd ....
9th	24th ....
10th	25th ....
11th	26th ....
12th	27th ....
13th	28th ....
14th	29th ....
15th	30th ....
31st	

SEPTEMBER

1st	16th ....
2nd	17th ....
3rd	18th ....
4th	19th ....
5th	20th ....
6th	21st ....
7th	22nd ....
8th	23rd ....
9th	24th ....
10th	25th ....
11th	26th ....
12th	27th ....
13th	28th ....
14th	29th ....
15th	30th ....

OCTOBER

1st	16th ....
2nd	17th ....
3rd	18th ....
4th	19th ....
5th	20th ....
6th	21st ....
7th	22nd ....
8th	23rd ....
9th	24th ....
10th	25th ....
11th	26th ....
12th	27th ....
13th	28th ....
14th	29th ....
15th	30th ....

31st ....

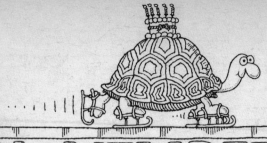

NOVEMBER

1st	16th ....
2nd	17th ....
3rd	18th ....
4th	19th ....
5th	20th ....
6th	21st ....
7th	22nd ....
8th	23rd ....
9th	24th ....
10th	25th ....
11th	26th ....
12th	27th ....
13th	28th ....
14th	29th ....
15th	30th ....

DECEMBER

1st	16th ....
2nd	17th ....
3rd	18th ....
4th	19th ....
5th	20th ....
6th	21st ....
7th	22nd ....
8th	23rd ....
9th	24th ....
10th	25th ....
11th	26th ....
12th	27th ....
13th	28th ....
14th	29th ....
15th	30th ....
	31st ....

WHO GETS WHICH
BIRTHDAY PRESENT?

BIRTHDAY

It's my birthday today,
And I'm nine.
I'm having a party tonight,
And we'll play on the lawn
If it's fine.
There'll be John, Dick and Jim,
And Alan and Tim,
And Dennis and Brian and Hugh;
But the star of the show,
You'll be sorry to know,
Will be Sue.
(She's my sister, aged two,
And she'll yell till she's blue
In the face, and be sick).

Anon.

GIVE A COLOUR PARTY

Tired of the same old party round? Strike out and throw a colour party!

They are best held in the evening, and the colour you choose can determine what sort of party you will have. Here are some ideas for holding a green party and a pink one. One word of caution – the only colour that doesn't work for food is blue – somehow it looks offputting rather than inviting.

THE GREEN PARTY
Send out the invitations on green paper, written in green ink, and ask everyone to come dressed in green. As the party giver you must show the way. If you can find some green hair-colour and fabric colour, you should be able to make yourself green from head to toe.

Make the invitation fun:

> Come and help Ben 'Green' Smith
> celebrate his green birthday party
> on October 11. Only those wearing
> green will be admitted.
> Time: 6.00 Place: The Green Smiths
> Carriages: 8.30 Dress: Anything green.

Decorate the room with green balloons and streamers, and put green bulbs in the lights. Make a tape to play green music. (Green grow the rushes, oh! Greensleeves, Ten Green Bottles, The Wearing of the Green, Green Door, The Green Green Grass of

Home, anything written by Verdi – work that one out! You'll have got the general idea.) See how many of the tunes your friends can identify, and give a prize (green, of course) to the one who does best.

Cover the table with a green cloth, and use green candles, green cardboard plates and cups. Decorate the table with little posies of green.

Play one or two games, or have a disco going as the guests arrive before they get down to the serious business of the green buffet.

Starters: Pineapple and Cheese chunks on cocktail sticks (dye the pineapple green with food colouring) stuck into half a cabbage. You can also buy green cocktail cherries and onions.

Pinwheel sandwiches: make these with green herby butter, cream cheese coloured green and mixed with chopped celery or chives.

Sausages on sticks can be slightly green if you choose the herby ones, and have some green mustard to dip them in.

Colour dips for crisps a light green – and have lots of celery and pepper (green) sticks to dip as well.

Main Course: Gammon and Green Pineapple (dyed with green vegetable dye); Potato Moussaka* with cheesy-green potato topping; Spaghetti Bolognese with green pasta.

Pudding. Tiny meringues coloured green and served with pistachio ice-cream. A green fruit salad with grapes, kiwi fruit, green pineapple, apple, bananas (which dye easily if you put a few drops of green in the lemon juice when you slice the bananas). Have some plain ice-cream on hand too. Not everyone likes pistachio. Gooseberry fool*.

Drinks: Colour them all green and call them Jungle wine.

If everyone is still on their feet after this little lot, bring on the music and start the games again.

Green Jungle Wine.

THE PINK PARTY

Follow the instructions for the green party, but decorate the table with pink candles and pink flowers. Pink light bulbs cast a gentle glow, so you can't count on them for so much help! Make a tape of pink music to play as your guests arrive to get into the mood (the soundtrack of Pretty in Pink, Lily the Pink, the music of Pink Floyd, Mighty Like a Rose, Der Rosenkavalier, La Vie en Rose). A pink prize to the guest who identifies the greatest number of titles. Play one or two games, or get the disco started before your guests begin their pink buffet.

Starters: Pinwheel sandwiches: make them pink by using pink butter (butter and tomato ketchup) and cream cheese coloured with ketchup. You can add minced ham as well.

Sliced ham rolled round pink cream cheese and cut into bite-sized pieces and speared on cocktail sticks, with red cocktail cherries. Stick them into half a red cabbage.

Pink coloured dips, with strips of red pepper and radishes to dunk.

Little grilled sausages with bacon wrapped round them and grilled again.

Main Course: Gammon and pink pineapple; Potato moussaka* with pink cheesy-potato topping; Spaghetti Bolognese with tomato flavoured (orangey-pink) spaghetti. A selection of cold meats and salad – ham, tongue, salami, liver sausage, spam, turkey, chopped ham. The salad can be made with red lettuce, tomatoes, radishes and red pepper (a red salad rather than a pink one, but the feeling is there!).

Chopped pickled beetroot in sour cream.

Pickled red cabbage.

A selection of fishy things with pink/red salad; taramasalata; prawns, tinned or fresh salmon; tuna fish.

Pudding: Pink fruit salad made with pink grapefruit, strawberries, raspberries, cherries, guavas, with pink whipped cream.

Rhubarb fool* with pink wafer biscuits.

Pink meringues with pink ice cream – raspberry or strawberry.

Drinks: Colour orange juice with grenadine syrup, lemonade with pink colouring and call them Pink Lady and Pink Champagne.

NB Cochineal is lethally strong, so watch how much you use. If disastrous, call it a red party!

* recipes on p. *94*

THE PERFECT HOST
– My worst birthday –
by Tony Robinson

Warning–Those who have a delicate stomach should turn swiftly to the next page but one.

My worst birthday party was the one when I poisoned all the guests. At least, everyone says it was me. They say I should never have done the cooking with a septic finger – especially kneading the pizza dough. But what I say is, it was my good hand that did the kneading while I held the dough down with the other elbow. And anyway, even if my bad finger did actually touch the dough for a quarter of a micro-second when I was picking it up off the floor, no germs could have leapt across and set up a refugee camp on the anchovies because I'd had the elastoplast round the finger for days.

Illness strikes different people in different ways, doesn't it? One bloke, who I'd never seen before but I think was somebody's boyfriend, tried to eat the garden furniture. Honestly! He bit lumps out of the legs of the nice garden chairs we'd bought in the John Lewis sale – and we'd only had them a week. Someone else was lying on the kitchen floor singing a selection of popular songs from the sixties. I know people do that at most grown-ups' parties, but they don't usually change colour the way he did – from green to white to blue like Martian traffic lights.

There were hordes of frenzied party-goers hammering on the bathroom door, but whoever had got there first seemed to be going for some sort of world record; someone on the landing was administering the kiss-of-life — at least I assume that's what she was doing; all around me there were people clutching their stomachs and rolling into balls like woodlice. I couldn't believe it! What a fuss over a bit of salmonella.

But I didn't lose my cool. I remained the perfect host, cracking jokes, pulling party poppers, passing round the pizza . . .

Later, when the last ambulance had gone and I'd finished shampooing the carpet, I was able to flop into the armchair and look back on the day's events. I may have lost a few friends, some of them permanently, but as long as everyone had had a good time, that's all that mattered, wasn't it?

And look, there was three-quarters of a pizza left. I could have it all to myself.

MY DREAM PARTY

If I could have any birthday party I wanted, it would be like this.

It would be on .... (date)

The weather would be ....

I'd invite ....

....

I'd wear ....

We'd eat ....

The special event would be ....

I'd play this music ....

I'd like these presents ....

....

I'd like to give everyone at the end ....

....

I'd have the party in ....

It would start at .... and go on until ....

This is my birthday cake:

MY BEST – AND WORST – BIRTHDAY
by Gyles Brandreth

My best and worst birthdays came on the same day, March 8, 1958, the day I turned 10. When I was 9 I was a little short for my age, but it didn't worry me too much because I was convinced that on my 10th birthday I would wake up and find myself a whole lot taller. Unfortunately the morning dawned. I threw myself out of bed and ran down to the kitchen to measure myself against the side of the refrigerator. My height the night before had been marked up on the fridge door. My height this morning was – believe it or not, exactly the same. If anything, in fact, I was a millimetre shorter! I was as miserable as a skunk in a perfume factory, until I opened my first birthday card and read in it a poem that boosted me right away, and has kept me going over the last thirty years.

This is it:

> *Don't worry if your size is small*
> *And your rewards are few,*
> *Remember that the mighty oak*
> *Was once a nut like you!*

BETWEEN BIRTHDAYS

My birthdays take so long to start.
They come along a year apart.
It's worse than waiting for a bus;
I fear I used to fret and fuss,
But now, when by impatience vexed
Between one birthday and the next,
I think of all that I have seen
That keeps on happening in between.
The songs I've heard, the things I've done,
Make my unbirthdays not so un-

Ogden Nash

WHICH OF THESE PRESENTS ARE IDENTICAL?

1.

2.

3.

4.

5.

6.

7.

8

9.

Answer: Presents 1 and 7 are identical.

PARTY GAMES

Lots of these games can be played both inside and outside.

PARTNERS
An ideal way to get your friends to mix is to pair them off as soon as they arrive. Then, for the rest of the party, whenever a partner is required, you have a ready-made pair.

Either cut out pictures of famous pairs of people from a magazine: Charles and Di, Tom and Jerry, Smith and Jones, or write the names of famous pairs on pieces of paper: Marks & Spencer, eggs and bacon, fish and chips, and give one part of each pair to your guests as they arrive. They have to go round looking for their partner.

HEADLINES (*pairs*)
For several weeks before your party, cut out big, recognisable pictures from the newspapers. Remove the captions, but make a careful note yourself of what they were. Pin the pictures up round the room and put a big number beside each one. Give each person a piece of paper with the numbers listed, and ask them to fill in the appropriate event, and what the headline was, or might have been. Prizes for those who come nearest the original and identify the event correctly.

MUSICAL KNEES (*pairs*)
When the music stops, stop dancing. One partner then sits on the other's knee. Any wobble and you're out.

Musical knees.

PASS THE PARCEL (*with forfeits*)
Make up the parcel with as many layers of paper as you have guests. When the music stops, whoever is holding the parcel has to unwrap one layer and perform a forfeit. Whoever gets to unwrap the final layer keeps the prize.

TEAM TICKLES (*two teams*)
You need two very long pieces of string each tied to a dessert spoon. The team leaders thread the spoon through their clothes DOWNWARDS, then pass the spoon to the next person, who threads it through their clothes UPWARDS, and so on. The first person must hang on grimly to the end of the string! The team that threads itself together first is the winner.

FEELY BOOTH
This is tremendous fun – particularly if you are having a Hallowe'en party. You need a freestanding screen. Either make one yourself, or ask an adult to make one for you. Heavy cardboard works well, if it is supported at each end. Cut four holes at waist height, just big enough to get your hand through comfortably. Fix strong plastic bags to the other side of the holes with strong sticky tape, staples or drawing pins. Make sure they will hold the weight of what you are going to put inside them. In the first

bag put some cold cooked spaghetti (if you put a teaspoonful of oil in the cooking water it will not stick to itself); in the second bag put a handful of peeled grapes; in the third bag put some firmly set jelly, roughly chopped; and in the fourth bag put some wire wool, or sawdust or a soapy wet sponge. You can vary the contents of the bags as much as you like. Then ask your guests to put their hands into the bags and identify what is inside.

NB The bags in the feely booth must be fixed so that you can reach the bottom of the bag easily, without being able to see what is in the bag if you look through the holes.

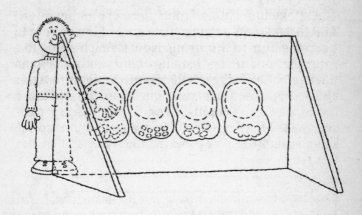

Feely Booth

CHOP THE CHOCOLATE

You will need:
 a large bar of chocolate or two; a pair of gloves; a hat; a
 scarf; a knife and fork; a dice and a cup

Sit your guests in a circle. Put the clothes, and the plate with the chocolate on it, and the knife and fork in the middle. Throw the dice in turn. The first person to throw a six dashes into the middle of the circle, puts on the clothes and tries to cut off a piece of chocolate. They carry on trying until someone else throws a six. The next one then rushes into the circle, puts on the clothes and starts cutting the chocolate, and so on. The game goes on as long as the chocolate lasts out.

BUN FIGHT

Cut sticky buns in half (one piece of bun per guest) and thread it on a string. Tie a knot at the bottom to keep the bun on the string. Now tie each string to a long piece of string, leaving about 30 cm between each one. Ask for two volunteers to hold the ends of the string. Then ask your guests to try and eat a piece of bun, keeping their hands behind their backs. NO CHEATING! The helpers can make life even more difficult by jerking the string a bit.

Bun Fight

Shoeing Horses

SHOEING HORSES (*teams of 4 people*)
You need one chair, and four plastic cups for each
team. Put the plastic cups at one end of the room
and the chair at the other. Blindfold each team
member in turn, and start them off at the end with
the plastic cups. They have to crawl up the room
with a cup, put it under one of the legs of the chair,
and crawl back and pick up another cup, until they
have a cup under each leg of the chair, or until they
have shod their horse. There is no rule that says
they can't steal a shoe from the other team's horse.
The other members of the team may call encourage-
ment, but not hand over cups or provide any other
help. The first team that manages to shoe its horse
wins.

GAMES FOR OUTSIDE ONLY

THE MATCHBOX HUNT

Give everyone a matchbox, and ask them to see how many different things they can cram into it in 2 minutes.

THROW THE WELLIE

You will need a wellie, and some old tyres or hoops. Lay the tyres or hoops out on the grass, and give each of them a value, 3, 5, 10, 20, 100. Draw a start line, and ask each person to throw the wellie into a hoop or tyre. Give them four goes. Highest score wins.

   If you don't have hoops or tyres, you can still play this game. Draw lines with pieces of tape or string, and give them different values. Then your guests have to see how far they can throw the wellie.

Warning You need plenty of space for this game – it's amazing how far a wellie can travel.

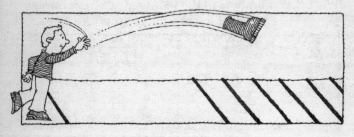

Throw the Wellie

ASSAULT COURSE

Again, you will need lots of space for this game. The difficulty of the course will depend on what you have available.

1 Throw a ball into a bucket so that it stays there.
2 Climb through a tyre (hanging up) or an open-ended barrel.
3 Run along a board balanced on two tyres, or straw bales (not too high off the ground).
4 High Jump – you can make a jump with three beanpoles and two clothespegs.
5 Long Jump – mark out the distance on the ground.
6 Run a certain distance with an egg and spoon.
7 Stepping Stones – place bricks in a line, or in an irregular pattern. If you put a foot on the ground you have to go back to the beginning and start again.
8 Cross the finishing line in a sack.

This is a good team game. First team to get home is the winner.

BANQUETS AND FEASTS

Everyone enjoys plenty of good things to eat on their birthday – or any other special occasion! Did you know that . . .

Thanksgiving Day is a big holiday in America. It's on the next-to-last Thursday in November, and it's traditional to eat roast turkey with cranberry sauce, pumpkin pie, and all sorts of other goodies.

The first Thanksgiving was in 1621. The smell of the turkeys roasting brought 90 friendly Indians to share the food prepared by the English settlers. There were 55 of them – only 4 were women, and they did all the cooking!

At the beginning of the last century, some English students in Paris were worried about not having a proper Christmas pudding to eat at Christmas. French food shops didn't stock such things – so they made up a prescription for a chemist! At that time chemists stocked eggs, raisins, etc. so could cope with a list of 'medicines' that included *Ova viii, Fruct. parv. Corynthii, zinziber pulv.* etc. The result? A splendid pudding, wrapped in parchment, on which was written in medical Latin, '*Apply the hot poultice to the affected part*'!

At a Christmas banquet in York in 1252, King Henry III ordered 600 roasted oxen to be served.

A single course at a banquet given by King Henry V included 'dates in composite, cream mottled, carp, turbot, tench, perch, fresh sturgeon with whelks, porpoise roasted, memis fried, crayfish, prawns, eels roasted with lamprey, a leche called the white leche flourished with hawthorne leaves and red haws, and a march pane . . .'

Feasts were popular in the Middle Ages! Very elaborate ones might have as many as 13 courses, each accompanied by appropriate entertainment, and served by up to 21 banquet officers, including cooks responsible for roasts, pastries, and sauces, a 'warner', who created wonderful table decorations, and a 'laverer', who supervised the washing of guests' hands.

Every month had its own special occasions to celebrate – some included St Valentine's Day, All Fool's Day, Midsummer's Day, Lammas Day, and St Catherine's Day.

President Loubet of France gave one of the biggest banquets ever, on 22nd September, 1900. He invited all 22,000 mayors in France, and their deputies. It's always been called 'le banquet des 100,000 maires'.

At the wedding of two Jewish cousins on Long Island, New York, in 1984, there were between 17,000 and 20,000 guests. The food included 2 tons of gefilte fish.

The most expensive menu at a banquet was served at a 5½ hour feast to celebrate 2500 years of Imperial Iran, in 1971. The guests ate quail eggs stuffed with caviare, a mousse of crayfish tails in Nantua sauce, stuffed rack of roast lamb, roast peacock stuffed with *foie gras*, fig rings and raspberry sweet champagne sherbet. The French wine cost £40 per bottle – you'd have to pay about £235 now!

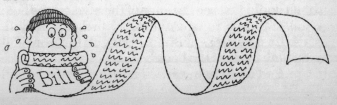

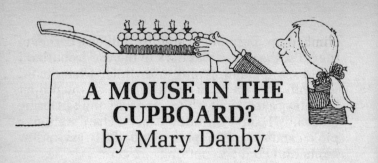

A MOUSE IN THE CUPBOARD?
by Mary Danby

For my first four birthdays there was no birthday cake. It was wartime, and eggs, butter and sugar were in short supply. I had seen pictures of birthday cakes with paper frills and coloured icing and little silver balls and candles. Fairy tale cakes.

A few days before my fifth birthday, I was in my bedroom doing nothing very much when I heard my mother arrive home from a visit to a neighbour. She came up the stairs, then I heard a door being softly opened. I looked out on to the landing and saw her carrying a large cardboard box into the spare room. In a little while she came out again, and seemed taken aback to see me in my bedroom doorway.

'Oh!' she said. 'Shall we go down and see what's for lunch?' She smiled brightly.

I had the impression she wanted to distract me from whatever was in the spare room, and decided not to ask about the cardboard box. Needless to say, however, at the first opportunity I went to investigate. There was a big wardrobe in the corner of the spare room, with hanging space on one side and shelves on the other. Right at the back of the top shelf I could just see the edge of the mysterious box. What could be in it? A birthday present? A doll, maybe, a new dress, with smocking on the front and a big bow to tie at the back?

I picked up a chair, carried it to the wardrobe and

climbed up. Very, very carefully, I lifted a corner of the lid of the box. It was dark in the wardrobe, but I could see something pink and white. Then the lid was off, and there in front of me was a proper birthday cake. It had white icing with pink lettering that said, 'Happy Birthday, Mary'. There were five pink candles and a pink paper frill. For a few moments I could do nothing but stare.

I had never tasted icing before. What if I were to pick off just a tiny piece? I pulled back the edge of the frill and pinched off a sticky white fragment. I can remember even now exactly how it tasted.

Between that day and my birthday, I must have visited the wardrobe at least ten times. Each time I would break off another small piece of my secret cake. I didn't see how anyone could possibly notice, as I always replaced the pink paper frill.

On my birthday, all my friends came round for tea. We ate our way through platefuls of fishpaste sandwiches, jam tarts and biscuits. Then, with a flourish, my mother produced the wonderful cake, and the 'oohs' and 'ahs' must have made the weeks of saving up her sugar ration worth while. The five candles were lit, and I blew them all out. Everyone sang 'Happy Birthday to You'. Then my mother said, 'You have to cut the cake and make a wish.'

To my horror, she began to unwrap the pink frill. There, revealed for all to see, was the line of little nibbles. But if anybody noticed, they were too well-brought-up to say so, thank goodness.

The cake was, as one of my friends put it, scrummy (short for 'scrumptious'), and it wasn't until the party was over and we were clearing up the mess that my mother turned to me and said brightly: 'Do you know, I believe we've had a little visitor in the spare room. Perhaps we ought to buy a mousetrap.'

CHECK THE DATE!
What famous or interesting event happened on *your* birthday?

JANUARY

1st The first car registration plate issued in Britain. A1 was a Napier car belonging to Earl Russell: 1904. **2nd** Louis Daguerre took the first photo of the moon, 1839. **3rd** J. R. R. Tolkien (author of *The Hobbit*) born, 1892. **4th** Jakob Grimm, collector of fairy tales, born 1785. **5th** First automatic ticket barrier on London underground installed, Stamford Brook, 1964. **6th** New Sadlers Wells Theatre opened, London, 1931. **7th** First railway station opened, at Mount Clare, Baltimore, USA, 1830. **8th** Elvis Presley born, 1935. **9th** First trial flight of supersonic plane *Concorde*, 1969. **10th** Penny Post system started, 1840. **11th** Charing Cross railway station opened, 1864. **12th** Charles Perrault, writer of fairy tales, born 1628. **13th** Labour Party founded 1893. **14th** Lewis Carroll (author of *Alice in Wonderland*) died 1898. **15th** First telephone directory published in London, 1880. It had 255 names in it. **16th** Ivan the Terrible, first Czar of Russia, crowned 1547. **17th** First ship crossed Antarctic Circle – Captain James Cook's *Resolution*, 1773. **18th** A. A. Milne (author of *Winnie-the-Pooh*) born 1882. **19th** First air raid casualties suffered – bombs were dropped on Great Yarmouth by the German L.3 Zeppelin, 1915. **20th** First Parliament including 'the Commons', 1265. **21st** *Concorde* began flying commercially, with simultaneous take-offs from London and Paris, 1976. **22nd** Spain ceded Falkland Islands to Britain, 1771. **23rd** US Navy bathyscape *Trieste* descended to a depth of 10,917 m in the Challenger Deep, Pacific, 1960. **24th** Gold discovered in California, 1848. **25th** The first winter Olympics: Chamonix, 1924. **26th** Sydney founded, 1788. The first troop of boy scouts formed, 1st Glasgow Boy Scout Troop, 1908. **27th** John Logie Baird gave the first public demonstration of television, 1926. **28th** Diet of Worms began, 1521. First motorist arrested for speeding! Doing 8 mph, he was arrested by a policeman on a bicycle, 1896. **29th** First petrol-driven car patented, built by Karl Benz, 1886. **30th** First purpose-built life-boat launched at South Shields, 1790. **31st** America's first earth satellite, *Explorer I*, launched from Cape Canaveral, 1958.

FEBRUARY

1st Bell Rock lighthouse started operating, 1811. **2nd** Alexander Selkirk, the real Robinson Crusoe, rescued, 1709. **3rd** First 'soft' landing on the moon, 1966. **4th** Sweet rationing ended, 1953. **5th** BBC pips heard for the first time, 1924. **6th** Women first allowed to vote in Parliamentary elections, 1918. Elizabeth II succeeds to throne, 1952. **7th** British Railways nationalised, 1940. **8th** Jules Verne, science fiction author, born 1828. **9th** Soap rationing began, 1942. **10th** Queen Victoria married Prince Albert, 1840.

11th Lowest UK temperature, −27.2°C (−17°F), Braemar, Scotland, 1895. **12th** The Australian gold rush began, 1851. **13th** Massacre of Glencoe, 1692. **14th** Eliza Armstrong was the first patient to be admitted to the Children's Hospital in Great Ormond Street, 1852. **15th** Decimal currency system began, 1971. **16th** Date of first cheque drawn on a British bank (cheque now owned by NatWest), 1659. **17th** International Red Cross founded, 1863. **18th** *Pilgrim's Progress*, by John Bunyan, published 1678. Planet Pluto discovered, 1930. **19th** Prince Andrew born, 1960. **20th** John Glenn first American to orbit earth, 1962. **21st** First demonstration of self-powered railway locomotive, 1804. **22nd** F. W. Woolworth opens first store in New York State, 1879. **23rd** Lawn tennis patented under name *Sphairistike*, 1874. **24th** Wilhelm Grimm, collector of fairy tales, born, 1786. **25th** Meat, butter, and other foods rationed, 1918. **26th** £1 notes first issued by the Bank of England, 1797. **27th** Goldie the Eagle escaped from London Zoo – recaptured a fortnight later, 1965. **28th** John Dunlop, aged 10, tried out his father's new invention: rubber tyres for his tricycle, made of garden hose filled with water, 1888. **29th** First Pulsar – pulsating radio source – announced in Cambridge, 1968.

MARCH

1st Yellowstone, oldest and largest National Park in America, was founded, 1872. **2nd** *Concorde*'s first flight, 1969. To protect the flight deck windows from supersonic speed, and cold as low as −150°C, they are coated with gold. **3rd** Munich introduced driving test for bicycle riders, 1895. **4th** The Forth Bridge opened, 1890. **5th** Covent Garden Theatre destroyed by fire, 1856. **6th** Frozen foods first went on sale, in America, 1930. **7th** Royal Horticultural Society founded by John Wedgwood (Josiah's son), 1804. **8th** Kenneth Grahame, author of *The Wind in the Willows*, born, 1859. **9th** Wedding of Napoleon Bonaparte and Josephine Beauharnais, 1796. **10th** First telephone message, 1876. **11th** Bradford reservoir in Sheffield burst – over 250 people drowned in flooding, 1864. **12th** 30 mph speed limit introduced, 1935. **13th** The planet Uranus discovered, 1781. **14th** New English Bible New Testament published, 1961. **15th** Selfridges department store opened, 1909. **16th** Highest rainfall ever recorded, at Cilaos, La Réunion, 1870 mm (73.52 ins), 1952. **17th** Kate Greenway, illustrator, born 1846. **18th** First walk in space, by Lieut. Col. Leonov from *Voshkod*, 1965. **19th** World's widest bridge opened, the 502.9 m (1650-ft) span Sydney Harbour Bridge, 1932. **20th** *Uncle Tom's Cabin* by Harriet Beecher Stowe published, 1852. **21st** London Planetarium opened, 1958. **22nd** Record 66 runners in Grand National, 1929. **23rd** Foundation stone of new Coventry Cathedral laid, 1956. **24th** Dead heat in the Boat Race, 1877. **25th** European Economic Community (the Common Market) formed, 1957. **26th** Driving tests for car owners introduced in Britain, 1934. **27th** First Rugby International, Scotland v England, played 1871. **28th** New Zealand makes lowest Test score ever, 26 against England, 1955. **29th** Queen Victoria opened Royal Albert Hall, 1871. **30th** Anna Sewell, author of *Black Beauty*, born 1820. **31st** Eiffel Tower opened, Paris, 1889.

APRIL

1st Royal Air Force formed, 1918. **2nd** Hans Christian Andersen, writer of fairy tales, born 1805. **3rd** 100th boat race won by Oxford, 1954. **4th** Francis Drake knighted by Queen Elizabeth I, 1581. **5th** First trials of driverless automatic trains on London Underground, 1964. **6th** Modern Olympic Games began, Athens, 1896. **7th** World Health Organisation started, 1948. **8th** Hour bell of Big Ben cast, 1858. **9th** National Gallery opened, 1838. **10th** Safety pin patented in America, 1849. **11th** Premiere of G. B. Shaw's *Pygmalion*, 1914. **12th** Union Jack became English flag, 1606. Yuri Gagarin first man in space, 1961. **13th** John Dryden became first Poet Laureate, 1668. **14th** Highway Code first issued, 1931. **15th** The 'unsinkable' *Titanic* hit an iceberg and sank, 1912. **16th** Royal yacht *Britannia* launched, 1953. **17th** Premium bonds started in Britain, 1956. **18th** Paul Revere's ride: the start of the American War of Independence, 1775. Start of first scout Bob-a-Job week, 1949. **19th** Miss Sweden wins first Miss World contest, 1951. **20th** First detective story published, *Murders in the Rue Morgue*, by Edgar Allan Poe, 1841. **21st** Rome founded, 753 BC. Queen Elizabeth II born, 1926. **22nd** Brazil discovered, 1500. **23rd** Order of the Garter founded, 1347. William Shakespeare born, 1564, and died, 1616. **24th** Biggest library in the world founded – United States Library of Congress, 1800. **25th** *Robinson Crusoe* by Daniel Defoe published, 1719. **26th** Wedding of King George VI and Queen Elizabeth, 1923. **27th** Regent's Park in London opened, 1828. **28th** Captain Cook reached Australia, 1770. **29th** Zip fastener patented in America, 1913. **30th** First live TV coverage of FA cup final, 1938.

MAY

1st The Great Exhibition opened by Queen Victoria, 1851. The Empire State Building completed, 1931. **2nd** Maiden voyage of QE2, 1969. **3rd** Lord Byron swims the Hellespont in Turkey in 70 minutes, 1810. **4th** General Strike started, 1926. Margaret Thatcher became Britain's first woman Prime Minister, 1979. **5th** Amy Johnson began her historic solo flight to Australia, 1930. First train robbery in the United States, 1865 (near North Bend, Ohio). **6th** First adhesive stamps, 1d. black and 2d. blue, officially issued by Post Office. Roger Bannister ran mile in under four minutes (3 mins 59.4 secs), 1954. **7th** Deaf composer Beethoven conducted first performance of his Ninth Symphony in Vienna, 1823. **8th** Coca-Cola appeared at Atlanta in Georgia, USA, 1886. World War II officially ended, 1945. **9th** J. M. Barrie, author of *Peter Pan*, born 1860. **10th** Home Guard established, 1940. **11th** First Siamese twins born, 1811. Chang and Eng were never separated. **12th** Edward Lear, author of many nonsense poems for children, born, 1812. **13th** Royal Flying Corps established, 1912. **14th** Louis XIV came to the throne of France, 1643, aged 4, and reigned for over 72 years. Edward Jenner made first vaccination against smallpox, 1796. **15th** Nylon stockings appeared for the first time in America, 1940. First flight of jet aircraft, 1941. **16th** 'Oscars' – Film Academy Awards – first presented, 1929. **17th** *Comic Cuts*, first comic, appeared in London, 1890. **18th** Napoleon Bonaparte proclaimed Emperor of France, 1804. **19th** Legion d'Honneur founded by Napoleon, 1802. **20th** Spanish Armada set sail from Lisbon, 1588. **21st** Charles Lindbergh, in *Spirit of St Louis* flew solo across Atlantic, 1927, in 33½ hours. **22nd** Wilbur Wright patented aeroplane, 1906. **23rd** Whipsnade Zoo opened, 1931. **24th** First Morse code message sent from Washington to Baltimore by inventor, Samuel Morse, 1844. **25th** Jesse Owens, American athlete, sets 6 world records in 45 minutes, 1935. After 6 years of building, the new Coventry Cathedral consecrated, 1962. **26th** First hippo arrived in Britain, 1850. First Le Mans 24-hour race, 1923. **27th** Golden Gate Bridge, San Francisco, opened, 1937. **28th** The longest sea dam in the world, the Afsluitdijk, completed, running over 32.5 km across the mouth of the Zuider Zee in Holland, 1932. **29th** Edmund Hillary and Sherpa Tenzing were the first men to climb Everest – reaching the top 11.30 a.m., 1953. **30th** The Theatre Royal, Bristol, oldest theatre still in use in Britain, opened, 1766. **31st** Big Ben first began recording time, 1859.

JUNE
1st Television licences, costing £2, first issued in Britain, 1946. **2nd** Coronation of Queen Elizabeth II, 1953. **3rd** *Gemini 4* launched – during flight, Ed White became first American to walk in space. **4th** First 'Trooping of the Colour', 1805. **5th** In a referendum asking British citizens if they wanted to join the Common Market, the winning vote was YES, 1975. **6th** The Ashmolean, Oxford, became first museum to open in Britain, 1683. **7th** BBC radio serial *The Archers* started, 1950. **8th** The next transit of Venus across the face of the sun, 2004. **9th** Hong Kong leased by Britain from China for 99 years, 1898. **10th** SOS signal transmitted for first time when liner *Slavonia* wrecked off the Azores, 1909. Biro patented, 1943. **11th** Oil first pumped ashore from North Sea oilfields, 1975. **12th** Baseball invented by Abner Doubleday, 1839. **13th** The Queen's official birthday. **14th** The 'Stars and Stripes' became flag of the USA, 1777. **15th** King John sealed Magna Carta at Runneymede, 1215. **16th** Russian Valentina Tereshkova became first woman in space, 1963. **17th** Decimal postage stamps went on sale, 1970. **18th** Battle of Waterloo, 1815. **19th** London Metropolitan Police, Britain's first police force, founded by Sir Robert Peel, 1829. **20th** Queen Victoria came to the throne, 1837. **21st** Work began on rebuilding St Paul's Cathedral after the Fire of London, 1675. **22nd** First cricket match at Lord's, 1814. **23rd** William Penn signed treaty of peace and friendship with Indians, 1683. **24th** Training of nurses in Britain started at St Thomas's Hospital, London, 1860. **25th** Custer's Last Stand – Sioux Indians led by Crazy Horse beat the American cavalry at Little Big Horn in Montana, 1876. The only cavalry survivor was a horse, Comanche. **26th** Automobile Association formed, 1905. **27th** Disguised as a girl, Bonnie Prince Charlie escaped over the sea to Skye, 1746. **28th** Queen Victoria's coronation, 1838. **29th** *Daily Telegraph* first published 1895. Great Comet sighted, 1861. **30th** Charles Blondin crossed Niagara Falls on a tightrope, 1859.

JULY

1st 999 emergency telephone service started, 1937. **and** The Salvation Army founded by William Booth, 1865. **3rd** World's first colour TV transmission, London, 1928. **4th** Statue of Liberty presented to America by France, 1884. First London bus ran from Marylebone Road to Bank, 1829. **5th** World's first speed limit imposed in Britain, 1865. **6th** First photograph of lightning taken by Robert Haensel in Bohemia (now Czechoslovakia), 1883. **7th** The liner *United States* made the fastest ever Atlantic crossing – 5465 km in 3 days, 10 hours and 40 minutes, 1952. **8th** Hottest day recorded in London – 98°F, 36.6°C, 1808. Total eclipse, 1842. **9th** First Lawn Tennis Championships, Wimbledon, 1877. **10th** Parking meters came into operation for the first time in England, 1958. **11th** First transatlantic TV by satellite (*Telstar 1*) from USA to France, 1962. **12th** Panama Canal officially opened, 1920. **13th** Start of World Cup Football competition – first winner, Uruguay, 1930. **14th** The Bastille, destroyed during French Revolution, 1789. The day is now a French holiday. **15th** Margarine patented in France, 1869. **16th** *Apollo II* launched with Neil Armstrong, Edwin Aldrin and Michael Collins, 1969. **17th** Queen opened Humber Estuary Bridge, the longest single-span structure in the world, 1981. **18th** Highest recorded rainfall in UK: 280 mm (11 ins) at Martinstown, Dorset, 1955. **19th** *Mary Rose*, Henry VIII's warship, sank in the Solent, 1545. **20th** Euston station, the first in London, opened, 1837. **21st** Neil Armstrong first man on moon, 1969. **22nd** Highest recorded UK temperature: 38.1°C (100.5°F) Tonbridge, Kent, 1868. First solo round-the-world flight completed – Wiley Post flew 15,596 miles (25,099 km) in 7 days, 18 hrs, 49 mins, 1933. **23rd** Twelve ringers from Ecclesfield School, Sheffield, achieved a world record handbell recital – 56 hrs, 3 mins, 1985. **24th** The Speaking Clock (TIM) began, 1936. **25th** Louis Blériot made first flight across English Channel in 36.5 mins, 1909. **26th** Prince Charles became Prince of Wales, 1958. **27th** First flight of the *Comet*, world's first jet airliner, 1949. **28th** First potatoes arrived in Britain, 1586. Beatrix Potter born, 1866. **29th** Spanish Armada defeated off Plymouth, 1588. **30th** Penguin paperbacks went on sale, 1935. **31st** David Scott and James Irwin first men to ride on moon, using Lunar Roving Vehicle, 1971.

AUGUST

1st First metric weight, the kilogram, introduced in France, 1793. **2nd** *Alice's Adventures in Wonderland* published 1865. It only sold 48 copies. **3rd** Christopher Columbus began voyage during which America discovered, 1492. **4th** Britain declared war on Germany, 1914. **5th** Cornerstone of Statue of Liberty laid, 1884. **6th** The sandwich invented – a slice of beef between two pieces of bread, ordered by the Earl of Sandwich, 5 a.m. 1762. **7th** First Royal Ascot horse race meeting, 1711. **8th** First Davis Cup competition – USA won! – 1900. **9th** Leonidas and Greek army defeated by

Persians at Thermopylae, 480 BC. **10th** Foundation stone of Greenwich Observatory laid, 1675. **11th** Child chimney sweeps banned, 1840. **12th** Last quagga in the world died in Artis Zoo, Amsterdam, 1883. **13th** Battle of Blenheim, 1704. **14th** World War II ended with surrender of Japan, 1945. **15th** Berlin founded, 1237. **16th** Tate Gallery opened, 1897. **17th** *Eagle II*, the first transatlantic balloon, landed in France, 1978. **18th** Virginia Dare born, the first child of settlers in the New World, 1587. **19th** Bonnie Prince Charlie claimed the throne of Britain, 1745. **20th** Ascent of River Niger by British steamships *Albert*, *Wilberforce* and *Soudan* began, 1841. **21st** An Italian waiter stole Leonardo da Vinci's *Mona Lisa* from the Louvre, 1911. **22nd** Start of the Civil War in England, between forces of Charles I and Parliament, 1642. **23rd** Blitz began with an all-night raid on London, 1940. **24th** Vesuvius erupted, burying Pompeii and Herculaneum under mud and ash, AD 79. **25th** Captain Matthew Webb first person to swim English Channel: 22 hours, 1875. **26th** Longbows used for the first time in war at the battle of Crecy; the English defeated the French, 1346. **27th** Krakatoa, a volcanic island between Sumatra and Java, erupted, 1883. **28th** Severe earthquake in Mexico: over 500 people killed, 1973. **29th** Battleship *Royal George* sank at anchor at Spithead, with the loss of over 900 lives, 1782. **30th** British Factory Act regulating employment of children passed, 1833. **31st** Siege of Leningrad started, 1941.

SEPTEMBER

1st Henry VI became king, aged 9 months. His first decree signed with a thumb-print gave his nurse the right to punish him 'reasonably from time to time', 1422. **2nd** Great Fire of London started, 1666. **3rd** Britain and France declared war on Germany (start of World War II), 1939. **4th** Los Angeles in California founded, 1781. **5th** Canterbury Cathedral destroyed by fire, 1174. **6th** Ferdinand Magellan's ship *Vittoria* arrived in Spain after first circumnavigation of the world, 1522. **7th** Grace Darling rescued crew of the shipwrecked *Forfarshire*, 1838. **8th** The Dutch settlement of New Amsterdam seized and renamed New York, 1664. **9th** Soap rationing ended in Britain, 1950. **10th** George Smith, a London taxi-driver, was first person convicted of drunken driving, 1897. **11th** The WI (Women's Institute) first started in Britain in Anglesey, 1915. **12th** Cleopatra's Needle, a 20.88 m high Egyptian obelisk, erected on the Thames Embankment, 1878. **13th** World record temperature recorded at Al'azizyah in Libya – 58°C (136.4°F), 1922. **14th** First direct hit on the moon by Russian space probe *Lunik II*, 1959. **15th** First use of tanks in World War I, at Flers, 1916. **16th** The Pilgrim Fathers set sail from Plymouth in the *Mayflower*, 1620. **17th** 33⅓ LP records launched in New York, 1931. **18th** First illuminations in Blackpool, 1879. **19th** First 'manned' hot-air balloon flight – the crew were a sheep, a duck, and a cockerel, France, 1783. **20th** Ferdinand Magellan sailed from Spain with 5 ships on the first expedition round the world, 1519. **21st** France declared a republic, 1792. **22nd** Sir Robert Walpole first Prime Minister to live at 10 Downing Street, 1735. **23rd** Planet Neptune discovered, 1846. **24th** First dirigible flown by Henri Giffard from Paris to

Trappe, 1852. It was 45 m long, 12 m diameter, and flew at just over 6 mph. **25th** Vasco Balboa became first European to see Pacific Ocean, 1513. **26th** Francis Drake reached Plymouth in the *Golden Hind* after first British circumnavigation of the world, 1580. **27th** First public train service ran 27 miles from Darlington to Stockton, 1825. **28th** First Marks and Spencer opened in Manchester, 1894. **29th** Battle of Marathon, 490 BC. Miguel de Cervantes, author of *Don Quixote*, born 1547. **30th** BBC Radio 1 broadcast for the first time, with *The Breakfast Show*, 1967.

OCTOBER

1st Disney World, the largest amusement park in the world, opened in Florida, 1971. **2nd** First rugby match played at Twickenham (Harlequins v Richmond), 1909. **3rd** SOS (Save Our Souls) established as an international distress signal, 1906. **4th** First public escalator opened at Earls Court Underground, 1911. **5th** The Jarrow March of unemployed shipyard workers began, 1936. **6th** First ever talking picture shown in America, 1927. **7th** First photo of the far side of the moon transmitted by Russia's *Lunik III* space probe, 1959. **8th** First street collection for charity – Lifeboat Day – in Britain, 1891. **9th** Captain Cook first set foot on New Zealand, 1769. **10th** Volcanic eruption on Tristan da Cunha, 1961. Entire population evacuated to Britain. **11th** The *Mary Rose* raised, 1982. **12th** Columbus discovered America (the island of San Salvador) 1492. **13th** First Merseyside 'derby' between Everton and Liverpool played, 1894. **14th** Battle of Hastings, 1066. **15th** First human flight in a balloon made by Jean de Rozier, Paris, 1783. **16th** The Houses of Parliament burned down, 1834. **17th** Children Amala and Kerala, found living with wolves in India, 1930. **18th** Rules for American football drawn up in New York, 1873. **19th** Sir Humphry Davy announced discovery of sodium, 1807. **20th** Lieut. Harold Harris first person whose life was saved by using a parachute, 1922. **21st** Battle of Trafalgar – Lord Nelson and the British navy beat the French and Spanish fleets, 1805. **22nd** First parachute descent was made, over Parc Monceau in Paris, 1797. **23rd** The world was created today (on Sunday at 9.00 a.m., 4004 BC) according to 17th century Archbishop Ussher of Armagh. **24th** The United Nations formally came into existence, 1945. **25th** The Charge of the Light Brigade! Crimean War, 1854. **26th** The Football Association started, 1863. **27th** Garibaldi began march on Rome, 1867. **28th** The Statue of Liberty unveiled, 1886. **29th** International Red Cross founded, 1863. **30th** Fire at the Tower of London, 1841. **31st** Zebra crossings introduced in Britain, 1951.

NOVEMBER

1st The Pony Club founded in Britain, 1929. **2nd** First crossword appeared in a British newspaper (the *Sunday Express*), 1924. **3rd** Half of the 5.18 m, 16 tonne statue of Lord Nelson hauled into position on top of Nelson's column in Trafalgar Square, 1843. **4th** The other half of Nelson's statue hauled into position, 1843. **5th** Guy Fawkes' attempt to blow up Parliament (the Gunpowder Plot) foiled, 1605. **6th** Abraham Lincoln elected president of USA, 1860. **7th** Canadian Pacific Railway completed, 1885. **8th** X-rays discovered by Wilhelm Röntgen, 1895. **9th** Britain's first woman mayor elected, Aldeburgh, 1908. **10th** Stanley met Livingstone at Ujiji, 1871. **11th** The Armistice, ending World War I, signed 1918. First Poppy Day, 1921. **12th** First photo of the Loch Ness monster taken, 1933. **13th** Robert

Louis Stevenson, author of *Treasure Island*, born, 1851. **14th** Colour programmes began on British TV, 1969. **15th** Sir Isaac Pitman's system of shorthand published, 1837. **16th** Greatest meteor shower of historic times, visible in northern latitudes of Pacific, fell on night of 16 – 17 Nov, 1966. **17th** Elizabeth I came to the throne, 1558. **18th** St Peter's Church in Rome consecrated, 1626. **19th** Abraham Lincoln delivered Gettysburg Address, 1863. **20th** Princess Elizabeth (later Queen Elizabeth II) married Prince Philip, 1947. **21st** The phonograph invented by Thomas Edison, 1877. **22nd** Vasco da Gama first known person to round the Cape of Good Hope, 1497. **23rd** First jukebox installed, in Palais Royal Saloon, San Francisco, 1889. **24th** Frost Fair with roasted oxen, on frozen Thames, 1715. **25th** The Mousetrap – world's longest-running play – opened, 1952. **26th** Tomb of the pharaoh Tutankhamun discovered, 1922. **27th** William Shakespeare married Anne Hathaway, 1582. **28th** Lady Astor became first woman MP in Britain, 1919. **29th** Lousia May Alcott, author of *Little Women*, born, 1832. **30th** The first football international – England and Scotland drew 0-0, 1872.

DECEMBER

1st British Post Offices issued first special Christmas stamps, 1966. **2nd** Rebuilt after the Great Fire, St Paul's Cathedral was opened, 1697. **3rd** First heart transplant operation, 1967. **4th** First publication of *The Observer*, the oldest Sunday newspaper in the UK, 1791. **5th** The brig *Marie Celeste* found abandoned, 1872. What happened to the crew has never been discovered. **6th** Columbus discovered Hispaniola (now Haiti) 1492. **7th** William Pitt the Younger, aged 24, became Britain's youngest Prime Minister, 1783. **8th** First woman appeared on the British stage, 1660 (as Desdemona in Shakespeare's *Othello*). **9th** First episode of *Coronation Street*, 1960. **10th** Nobel prizes first awarded, 1901. **11th** James II fled from Britain, 1688. Edward VIII abdicated, 1936. **12th** The hovercraft patented, 1955. **13th** New Zealand discovered by Abel Tasman, 1642. **14th** Roald Amundsen led the first successful team to reach the South Pole, 1911. **15th** Nylon was first produced commercially in America, 1939. **16th** The Boston Tea Party took place – an American protest against British taxation, 1773. **17th** The Wright brothers made the first aeroplane flight, 1903. **18th** Slavery abolished in the USA, 1865. **19th** Death of Walter Williams, claimed to be the last American Civil War veteran, aged 117, 1959. **20th** First atomic-powered ice-breaker, the *Lenin*, began operating. **21st** The Pilgrim Fathers landed in Massachusetts, 1620. **22nd** 70 mph speed limit began in Britain, 1965. **23rd** BBC began daily radio news broadcasts, 1922. **24th** Largest meteorite to fall in Britain landed at Barwell, Leicestershire, total weight at least 46.25 kg, 1965. **25th** William the Conqueror crowned at Westminster Abbey, 1066. **26th** Radium discovered by Pierre and Marie Curie, 1898. **27th** First performance of *Peter Pan*, by J. M. Barrie, 1904. **28th** Highest recorded cricket innings score – 1107 runs, by Victoria v New South Wales, 1926. **29th** Heavy water discovered, 1931. **30th** Rudyard Kipling, author of *Just So Stories* and *The Jungle Books*, born, 1865. **31st** Chimes of Big Ben first broadcast, 1923.

HORRORSCOPE

Libra: LIBRArians
Librarians are usually charming people, helpful, and full of interesting information. But beware! Underneath that friendly exterior can be found a MONSTER! If you don't return a book you've borrowed when they expect it, librarians will stop smiling, and may start snarling. They will pursue you relentlessly wherever you go until you have paid the PENALTY! You cannot escape . . .
Good Advice: be nice to Librarians.

Virgo: VIRaGO
Long ago, Viragos were heroines (and sometimes heroes). Brave and noble, they liked dangerous quests and difficult adventures. But as dragons became scarcer, and lost treasures found, Viragos have found fewer things to be heroic about. Restless, energetic, always looking for a challenge, they are just the people to help if you have some special venture on hand – but don't waste their time, or they can lose their tempers! Viragos are particularly brave going to the dentist, cleaning up after everyone else, and explaining just how the window got broken.
Good Advice: to have a Virago as a friend.

Taurus: MinoTAURUS
People who are half human and half not can be interesting to know. Do not worry if a Minotaurus wants to play at mazes. They enjoy puzzles and conundrums. Always carry a piece of string if you have a Minotaurus friend: it's useful for marking routes, and you can always play cats cradle. Minotauruses are good at chasing and tracking, but don't wave rags at them. They get annoyed if you do.
Good Advice: don't take bulls into china shops.

Aries: vARIES
Varies people tend to change their minds. Sometimes they can't make up their minds at all. Don't be misled and associate them with sheep. Varies aren't at all woolly. Sometimes they just want to consider a thing from every side. Sometimes a thing isn't worth deciding about. Sometimes they just enjoy considering. People who like thinking so much should be left to proceed at their own pace. It varies.
Good Advice: always try to see things from the other person's point of view.

Sagittarius: THE ARCHERS

Tough and energetic, Archers are always aiming at a target. They like the colour gold, and enjoy bulls-eyes. Some may detect agricultural overtones in the Archers. They talk a lot, and like radio better than television. If they get angry, they may fire at random (watch out!) and if they want to ignore something, they may bury themselves – under a haystack, a turnip clamp, the sofa cushions . . . Archers make good friends, and are excellent at hunting things down (give them all your obscurest homework – they'll love it!).

Good Advice: always have two strings to your bow.

Aquarius: MEREWOLVES

Merewolves are aquatic werewolves, only turning into wolves in meres, lakes, streams, the bath, etc. They are wonderfully good at anything watery – swimming, fishing, marine biology, hairdressing, water-colour painting: but in some cases they can only do their best work under water, and in wolf form. This can be most frustrating, so don't be surprised if they run about a lot howling and ravening (they are usually ravenous). Pat them on the head occasionally, and they will be very happy.

Good Advice: don't catch a wolf by its ears.

Cancer: ChANCERs

Chancers love living dangerously. They will take huge risks, *just* getting into class in time, gambling on getting the *last* helping of pudding, challenging Authority to notice that the rash is coloured in with felt-tips . . . And they usually get away with it! Take care if you're not a Chancer – if you're too close, wrath may descend on you instead. A very lucky sign, though when things do go wrong for a Chancer, it can be catastrophic!

Good Advice: make sure you have an alibi.

Scorpio: SCaRPers

Scarpers are never there when they're wanted, having amazing talents for lying low and keeping out of trouble (that includes jobs like washing-up). People born under this sign are good at running, hiding, and vanishing. Sometimes they become magicians and conjurers. Other good careers: anything to do with camouflage. Scarpers can have sharp tongues, and may, if roused, say stinging things.

Good Advice: shake your shoes out every day in case there's something nasty inside them.

A Camouflaged Scarper
↓

Leo: LEOtards

Leotards are strong, elegant and graceful, often fond of gymnastics, dancing, and exercise. They like to get things right – but they can become obsessive, ignoring their friends and being late because they are determined that their toes or fingers are going to be just right. Leotards can only be made to stretch a certain amount from their true shape before they snap back to their real selves. If you provoke them they will roar and turn very nasty.

Good Advice: let sleeping lions lie.

Pisces: PISKIES

Piskies are small, fast-moving (some people say they can't be seen at all), and very mischievous. Get on their right side, and they will be good friends for life. Cross them, and they will make your life very unpleasant. They are very good at finding lost things, they like the colour green, and prefer water to fire. They also enjoy a drink of milk last thing at night. There are many piskies in Cornwall.

Good Advice: a friend in need is a friend indeed.

Gemini: GrEMlINiS

These people are a bit mixed up! Usually twins, they are drawn irresistibly to machines, but they always manage to make the machines go wrong. Many people forget that Gremlinis come in pairs, mend one fault, and then wonder why the machine still won't go ... there is always a second thing wrong with it! Gremlinis have enquiring minds and don't mean to cause mechanical problems. Anger them, though, and they will do it deliberately! Try and keep them away from machines, or only give them simple, easily mendable ones to play with.

Good Advice: always carry a spanner.

Capricorn: GhOAsTS

GhOAsTS are the ghosts of goats. They can be extremely friendly, eating up any food that's around, keeping the grass down, providing warm fibres for knitting (though some say that jerseys knitted with ghostly goat wool are see-through and draughty). Ghoasts who don't feel appreciated at home may take to uttering long-drawn-out bleating noises on winter nights. This can be very alarming. After a couple of nights of this, most people give way, and do what the Ghoast wants. Ghoasts also like climbing. Have a few spare crags around.

Good Advice: carry a comb at all times.

CHOCOLATE CHARMERS

As a special treat, why not make each of your friends a little chocolate animal to decorate the table, or to take home. You can use this magic chocolate mixture for all of them. It sticks together very easily.

You will need:

1 Melt the chocolate in a double saucepan, or a bowl standing in a saucepan of boiling water – but don't let the water touch the mixture.
2 Warm the liquid glucose or golden syrup and mix well with the chocolate.
3 When cool wrap in clingfilm, put in a plastic bag or container and leave for at least one hour before using. When ready to start, knead the mixture *gently*.

To make a chocolate teddy bear
The body – Make a cone shape with about 20 gm (⅔ oz) of the mixture and flatten the top slightly.
The arms and legs – Make two sausages with 5 gm (⅙ oz) of mixture.
Make a dent with your little finger near one end and cut them in half, lengthways.
Turn up the feet and attach to the body. Mark claws with knife.

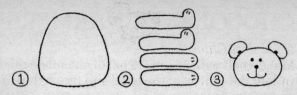

The head – Make a cone with 10 gm (⅓ oz). Cut mouth with a sharp knife and squeeze the side to make him smile.

Make indentations for the eyes and push in silver balls.

Attach two tiny balls for the ears. With your fingers supporting each ear, shape it.

Chocolate Cat

Make a cone with 15 gm (½ oz) of chocolate mixture.

Attach a long tapered sausage for the tail.

Make a 5 gm (⅙ oz) ball for the head.

Carefully pinch up the ears and the whiskers.

Make indentations and stick in silver balls for the eyes.

Add a tiny ball for the nose.

Mark the whiskers with a sharp knife.

Chocolate Chick

Make a ball with 15 gm (½ oz) of chocolate mixture.
Indent the centre for the head and pinch the sides to make wings.
Make a 5 gm (⅙ oz) ball for the head.
Make indentations for the eyes.
Using a sharp knife, make a small slit for the mouth and shape.
Gently squeeze the top of the ball to make a comb.
Make a cone for the tail and flatten it.
Make two cones for the feet and mark with the knife.

Scottie

Make a sausage with 15 gm (½ oz) of the chocolate mixture. Shape it into a curve and mark both ends with the knife for the legs. Pull up the tail.
Make a cube with 5 gm (⅙ oz) for the head, and slightly flatten one end. Pinch up the ears.
Make indentations for the eyes.
Pinch out the sides for whiskers and mark with the knife.
Cut a slit for the mouth.
Add silver balls eyes.
Add a tiny chocolate ball for the nose.

Dachshund

Make a sausage with 15 gm (½ oz) of mixture.

Make a tiny cone. Flatten it and attach it to the body for the tail.

Make 4 tiny sausages for the feet and attach them.

Make a 5 gm (⅙ oz) cone for the head. Make indentations for the eyes, and add a tiny ball for the nose.

Make two tiny cones for the ears. Flatten them and attach to the head.

Put in the silver eyes.

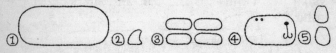

You can make lots of other animals using the same mixture. Why not try:

a rabbit   an owl   a tortoise

a mouse   a hippo   a frog

The mixture will keep for several weeks if it is wrapped in clingfilm and kept in a plastic container in a cool place.

(NB Baking chocolate can be bought at most supermarkets in slabs or buttons. Liquid glucose can be bought at most chemists. If the mixture is kneaded too much the ingredients will separate.

If the mixture becomes too soft, put it in a cool place until it becomes firm again.)

BIRTHDAY MIRTH

WHAT I'D GIVE MY FRIENDS IN THEIR TAKE-HOME BAGS

Presents I have given ....

....

Presents I am going to give ....

....

If I could give anything in the world, it would be ......

....

If I gave a book, it would be ....

If I gave some music, it would be ....

If I gave a toy, it would be ....

If I could give one magical present, it would be ....

....

MAKE A TAKE-HOME BAG

You will need: strong paper, 422 × 296 mm (A3), scissors, pencil, ruler, glue, ribbon.

You can use plain paper, which you can paint or decorate yourself, or patterned paper.

Measure a point 160 mm from each corner of the paper down the longest sides. There will be four points (see diagram).

Join opposite points, so that your paper is divided into three. The middle section will be rather smaller than the two outside sections.

Now draw a line two rulers' widths right down each long edge (see diagram).

Fold the paper across the *width* along the lines you have marked. This will make the sides and base of your bag. Flatten the paper out. Now fold along the *length* of the paper, and flatten the folds out. (This will form the ends of your bag.)

Cut the paper on the centre lines (see diagram). Turn the paper right side up. Glue one of the small centre sections between the cuts. Also glue a narrow strip, about 1 cm wide, down one of the long edges.

Fold the glued section up, and then fold the two sides of your bag over. Bend the long edges round, so that the bottom sticks to the glued section, and the glued strip overlaps and sticks to the unglued paper.

Repeat this on the other side, and leave your bag to dry. Glue a piece of ribbon about 15 cms long across the top of the bag to make a handle.

When the glue has dried, you can paint your bag,

or decorate it. How about labelling the bag with the name of the person who will receive it?

Note If you are going to put gold ingots, small elephants, or other exceptionally heavy presents in your bag, you should reinforce the seams and handles.

Use sticky tape along the seams. If you use a foil tape in a contrasting or complementary colour, it will make the bag look very smart.

To make stronger handles, use your scissors to cut a small slit in the paper on each side of the bag. Feed one end of the ribbon through the first slit, until about 1.5 cms protrudes on the inside of the bag. Tape this down very securely. Turn the bag round and do exactly the same thing on the other side (see diagram).

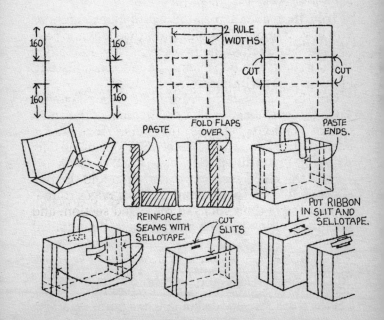

My hero's birthday

My hero is ....

His age is ....

His birthday is on ....

Sign of the zodiac ....

He is my hero because ....

He lives in ....

For his birthday I would like to give him ....

....

If I were invited to his birthday party, I'd wear ....

....

My hero's favourite food is ....

My hero's favourite sport is ....

Picture of my hero

The birthday card I'd like to send

Other important facts about my hero ....

....

My heroine's birthday

My heroine is ....

Her age is ....

Her birthday is on ....

Sign of the zodiac ....

She is my heroine because ....

She lives in ....

For her birthday I would like to give her ....

....

If I were invited to her birthday party, I'd wear ....

....

My heroine's favourite food is ....

My heroine's favourite sport is ....

Picture of my heroine
                    The birthday card I'd like to send

Other important facts about my heroine ....

....

POTATO MOUSSAKA

Moussaka is a Greek dish, and is traditionally made with aubergines, but lots of people find the taste of aubergine something they acquire later. As they are also expensive to buy it is probably a good idea to make a potato moussaka.

You will need:
5 large potatoes
50 gm plain flour
80 gm butter
200 gm minced beef
700 gm minced lamb
3 large onions, finely chopped
1 clove of garlic (if required)
½ litre tomato sauce (cheat and buy a tin)
2 bay leaves
1 tbsp oregano
½ tsp cinnamon
2 tbsp chopped parsley
¾ litre bechamel sauce (buy a packet or two to make the required amount)
100 gm grated cheese

To make:
1   Boil the potatoes and cut them into slices about 7 mm thick.
2   Cook the onions and the garlic (if you are using it) in some butter.

3 Add the minced beef and lamb and brown.
4 Add the tomato sauce, bay leaves, oregano, salt and pepper, cinnamon and chopped parsley, and cook until most of the liquid has evaporated.
5 Grease two large casseroles (or more if necessary) and layer the potato, meat, potato, meat, until you have used it all up, finishing with a layer of potato.
6 Colour the bechamel sauce either green or pink. Pour the coloured sauce over the top and sprinkle with the grated cheese.
7 Bake for 1 hour at 180°C/Mark 5 gas.

This dish is best the day after it is made. If you keep it in the fridge take it out at least two hours before you want to reheat it, and then heat for 30 – 45 mins.

FRUIT FOOL
You will need:
1 kilo of the fruit of your choice washed and ready to cook
3 tbsp water
170 gm caster sugar
½ litre double cream

To make:
1 Damp the saucepan and put in the fruit with 2 tbsp water.
2 Simmer gently for 10 mins.
3 Let the fruit cool, then push through a nylon sieve (use the back of a spoon) to make a puree.*
4 Whip the double cream until it is stiff.
5 Fold in the caster sugar.
6 Fold the cream into the puree and chill for several hours or overnight.

* If you want to make the colours strong add a few drops of food colouring.

HAPPY BIRTHDAY TO YOU!

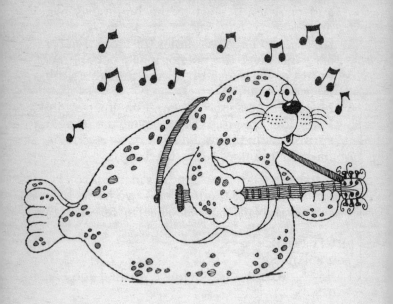

Answers to Jumbled Words, p. 29

PRESENTS   CELEBRATION   FRIENDS
SAUSAGES   WRAPPINGS   BIRTHDAYS
CAKE   GIFTS   PARTIES   GREETINGS CARDS
PARCELS   ENVELOPE   CHOCOLATE
ANNIVERSARY   ENTERTAINMENT